I Want a Pet

I Want a Goldfish

by Kimberly M. Hutmacher

Consulting Editor: Gail Saunders-Smith, PhD

Consultant: Jennifer Zablotny, DVM
Member, American Veterinary Medical Association

CAPSTONE PRESS
a capstone imprint

Pebble Plus is published by Capstone Press,
1710 Roe Crest Drive, North Mankato, Minnesota 56003.
www.capstonepub.com

Books published by Capstone Press are manufactured with paper
containing at least 10 percent post-consumer waste.

Library of Congress Cataloging-in-Publication Data
Hutmacher, Kimberly.
   I want a goldfish / by Kimberly M. Hutmacher.
      p. cm.—(Pebble plus. I want a pet)
   Includes bibliographical references and index.
   Summary: "Simple text and full-color photographs describe the responsibilities involved in caring for and choosing
a goldfish as a pet"—Provided by publisher.
   ISBN 978-1-4296-7597-0 (library binding)
   1. Goldfish—Juvenile literature. I. Title.
   SF458.G6H88 2012
   639.3'7484—dc23
                                                        2011021651

Editorial Credits
Erika L. Shores, editor; Bobbie Nuytten, designer; Sarah Schuette, studio stylist; Marcy Morin, studio scheduler;
   Kathy McColley, production specialist

Photo Credits
All photos by Capstone Studio/Karon Dubke, except Shutterstock: tristan tan, back cover

Note to Parents and Teachers

The I Want a Pet series supports common core state standards for English language arts related
to reading informational text. This book describes and illustrates goldfish ownership. The
images support early readers in understanding the text. The repetition of words and phrases
helps early readers learn new words. This book also introduces early readers to subject-specific
vocabulary words, which are defined in the Glossary section. Early readers may need assistance
to read some words and to use the Table of Contents, Glossary, Read More, Internet Sites, and
Index sections of the book.

Printed in the United States of America in North Mankato, Minnesota.
102011   006405CGS12

Table of Contents

Goldfish Are for Me

Shiny goldfish sparkle
as they dart through water.
Goldfish are interesting
to watch. Let's learn all about
owning these pets.

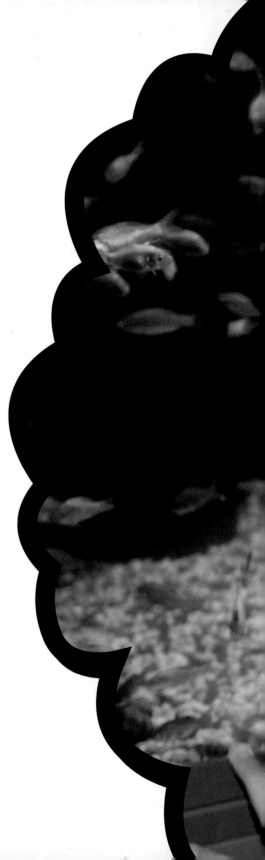

My Responsibilities

First decide where to keep your goldfish. Is there a spot for an aquarium? A tank that holds 5 to 10 gallons (19 to 38 liters) makes a good goldfish home.

You'll have to clean out

the tank every two weeks.

Goldfish get sick if their homes

get too dirty.

You'll feed your goldfish
each day. Follow the directions
on the food's label.
Too much food can make
fish unhealthy.

Choosing Your Goldfish

Ready for your own goldfish?
Buy goldfish from a good
pet store. Tanks should be clean.
The employees should be able
to answer your questions.

ICE BLUE CICHLID
$8.99

ACEI C

Look for healthy goldfish
with shiny skin and upright fins.
Your healthy fish should be
on the move!

KOI
$9.99

SHUBUNKIN, LARGE
$16.99

PLATINUM KOI
$9.99

COMET, LARGE
$9.99

TRAPDOOR SNAIL
$3.99

TADPOLE
$2.99

PET EXPO
WESLEY

PET EXPO

15

Buy an aquarium, gravel, and plants. Plants give goldfish places to hide.

Don't forget cleaning supplies.

You'll need to buy a filter,

air pump, net, and brush.

Goldfish live for 2 to 20 years.
With good care, your fish
will stay active and healthy
their entire lives.

Glossary

active—being busy and moving around

aquarium—a glass or plastic tank where pets, including fish, hamsters, and hermit crabs, are kept

employee—a person who works for and is paid by another person or business

filter—a machine in an aquarium that cleans water as it passes through

fin—a body part that fish use to swim and steer in water

gravel—a mixture of sand, pebbles, and broken rocks

healthy—fit and well; not sick

Read More

Ganeri, Anita. *Goldfish*. A Pet's Life. Chicago: Heinemann Library, 2009.

Kawa, Katie. *Colorful Goldfish*. Pet Corner. New York: Gareth Stevens Pub., 2011.

Stevens, Kathryn. *Fish*. Pet Care For Kids. Mankato, Minn.: The Child's World, 2009.

Internet Sites

FactHound offers a safe, fun way to find Internet sites related to this book. All of the sites on FactHound have been researched by our staff.

Here's all you do:

Visit *www.facthound.com*

Type in this code: 9781429675970

Check out projects, games and lots more at
www.capstonekids.com

Index

Word Count: 180
Grade: 1
Early-Intervention Level: 16